HARRY S. TRUMAN

PIVOTAL PRESIDENTS
Profiles in Leadership

HARRY S. TRUMAN

Edited by Kevin Geller

Britannica
Educational Publishing

IN ASSOCIATION WITH

ROSEN
EDUCATIONAL SERVICES

Published in 2018 by Britannica Educational Publishing (a trademark of Encyclopædia Britannica, Inc.) in association with The Rosen Publishing Group, Inc.
29 East 21st Street, New York, NY 10010

Copyright © 2018 by Encyclopædia Britannica, Inc. Britannica, Encyclopædia Britannica, and the Thistle logo are registered trademarks of Encyclopædia Britannica, Inc. All rights reserved.

Rosen Publishing materials copyright © 2018 The Rosen Publishing Group, Inc. All rights reserved.

Distributed exclusively by Rosen Publishing.
To see additional Britannica Educational Publishing titles, go to rosenpublishing.com.

First Edition

Britannica Educational Publishing
J.E. Luebering: Executive Director, Core Editorial
Andrea R. Field: Managing Editor, Compton's by Britannica

Rosen Publishing
Kathy Kuhtz Campbell: Senior Editor
Nelson Sá: Art Director
Brian Garvey: Series Designer
Alison Hird: Book Layout
Cindy Reiman: Photography Manager
Bruce Donnola: Photo Researcher
Supplementary material by Kevin Geller

Library of Congress Cataloging-in-Publication Data

Names: Geller, Kevin, editor.
Title: Harry S. Truman / editor Kevin Geller.
Description: First edition. | New York: Britannica Educational Publishing in Association with Rosen Educational Services, [2018] | Series: Pivotal Presidents: profiles in leadership | Includes bibliographical references and index. | Audience: Grades 7–12.
Identifiers: LCCN 2016053924 | ISBN 9781680486339 (library bound)
Subjects: LCSH: Truman, Harry S., 1884–1972—Juvenile literature. | Presidents—United States—Biography—Juvenile literature. | United States—Politics and government—1945-1953—Juvenile literature.
Classification: LCC E814 .H3327 2017 | DDC 973.918092 [B]—dc23
LC record available at https://lccn.loc.gov/2016053924

Manufactured in China

Photo credits: Cover, p. 3 (portrait), pp. 21, 31, 35, 45, 55 Bettmann/Getty Images; cover, p. 3 (background) Underwood Archives/Archive Photos/Getty Images; cover, pp. 1, 3 (flag) © iStockphoto.com/spxChrome; p. 6 Everett Collection Historical/Alamy Stock Photo; p. 11 Alfred Eisenstaedt/The LIFE Picture Collection/Getty Images; pp. 12, 57 Popperfoto/Getty Images; pp. 14, 19 Keystone-France/Gamma-Keystone/Getty Images; p. 16 Eliot Elisofon/The LIFE Picture Collection/Getty Images; p. 23 Harry S. Truman Library; pp. 24, 44 MPI/Archive Photos/Getty Images; pp. 27, 30 Thomas D. McAvoy/The LIFE Picture Collection/Getty Images; pp. 33, 37 Universal History Archive/Universal Images Group/Getty Images; p. 40 George Skadding/The LIFE Picture Collection/Getty Images; p. 42 Walter Sanders/The LIFE Picture Collection/Getty Images; p. 52 National Archives/Hulton Archive/Getty Images; p. 60 Marie Hansen/The LIFE Picture Collection/Getty Images; p. 63 © AP Images; p. 66 Dean Conger/Corbis Historical/Getty Images; interior pages flag Fedorov Oleksiy/Shutterstock.com.

Table of Contents

Introduction 6

Chapter 1 A Missouri Son 10

Chapter 2 A Soldier and a Politician 18

Chapter 3 First President from Missouri 28

Chapter 4 Postwar Challenges 39

Chapter 5 A Second Term 54

Conclusion 66
Glossary 68
For More Information 70
For Further Reading 75
Index 78

INTRODUCTION

Vice President Harry S. Truman (*left*) is sworn in as the thirty-third president of the United States on the evening of April 12, 1945. Truman's wife, Bess, solemnly witnesses the historic occasion.

It was late afternoon of a warm spring day. Vice President Harry S. Truman had just finished listening to a Senate debate. He was given a telephone message. It asked him to get to the White House as soon as possible. President Franklin D. Roosevelt had died suddenly of a cerebral hemorrhage at Warm Springs, Georgia, where he had gone for a short rest. That evening, April 12, 1945, at 7:09 p.m., Harry S. Truman took the oath of office as the thirty-third president of the United States. Later President Truman said to several White House newspapermen: "I feel as though the moon and all the stars and all the planets have fallen upon me. Please, boys, give me your prayers. I need them very much."

The new president faced many difficulties. The end of World War II was in sight, but American forces were still fighting in Europe and the Pacific. The people at home were supplying the needs of their own fighting forces and helping their Allies at a total cost of nearly $90 billion a year. An atomic bomb had been developed. It was the most powerful weapon the world had ever known. Truman knew that he must decide whether or not to use the bomb in the war with Japan.

Truman had to tackle these momentous challenges in the first months of his presidency. He came into office with great energy, helping to arrange Germany's surrender and then meeting with Allied leaders to discuss the fate of postwar Germany. He also sent a final demand to Japan to surrender or face "utter devastation." When Japan did not surrender, Truman authorized the dropping of atomic bombs on the cities of Hiroshima and Nagasaki. More than 100,000 men, women, and children were killed. This decision remains perhaps the most controversial decision ever made by a US president, one that scholars continue to debate today. Japan surrendered days after the bombs fell.

Victory and peace brought their problems, too. Soon after the end of World War II, a new crisis emerged as the Soviet Union began to expand communism into Eastern Europe. This was the start of the Cold War—a tense, decades-long rivalry between the Soviet Union and the United States. Truman led the country through the early years of the Cold War, pledging that the United States would fight the spread of communism throughout the world. This declaration—called the Truman Doctrine—was put to the test in

INTRODUCTION

1950, when communist North Korea invaded South Korea. Truman ordered US military forces to join the United Nations effort to help South Korea. The Korean War dragged on past the end of Truman's presidency.

Truman was plunged into the presidency at a key moment in US history. Readers of this book will understand the character, intellect, and politics that shaped this pivotal leader, one whom many scholars now rank among the country's best presidents.

Chapter 1

A Missouri Son

Harry S. Truman was a plainspoken Midwesterner from Missouri. For years he worked on his family's farm near Grandview, and it was this experience that cultivated one of his most enduring characteristics. "It was on the farm that Harry got his common sense," his mother, Martha Truman, once said. "He didn't get it in town." After he began a career in public service, many people noted how common sense was fundamental in even the most difficult decisions he made.

Truman's Family

Harry S. Truman was born on May 8, 1884, in Lamar, Missouri. He was the son of John Anderson Truman, a cattle trader and farmer, and Martha Ellen Young Truman. A younger brother, John Vivian Truman, called Vivian, was born in 1886, and a younger sister, Mary Jane Truman, followed in 1889.

Harry was named for his mother's brother, Harry Young. He was given the middle initial "S" (but no name) for his grandfathers, Anderson Shipp Truman and Solomon Young. Truman's great-grandmother, Nancy Tyler Holmes, was a first cousin of John Tyler, tenth president of the United States. It is interesting to know that Tyler was the first vice president to become president by succession (as stipulated by Article II, Section

Truman was born in this farmhouse in Lamar, Missouri. The pine tree *(left)* was planted on May 8, 1884, the day Harry was born.

Four-year-old Harry (*right*) poses with his two-year-old brother, Vivian, around 1888.

I of the US Constitution), and Truman was the seventh. It was Tyler who insisted that the vice president should actually become the president of the United States and not just acting president when he takes the office of the chief executive.

Boyhood

Shortly after Harry's birth, the Truman family moved to nearby Independence, Missouri, not far from Kansas City. There Harry attended grade school and high school.

In 1894 Harry and his brother came down with diphtheria, a bacterial infection marked by a sore throat, fever, a rapid pulse, and swollen neck glands. Mary Jane was sent to the farm in Grandview in the hope that she could avoid the disease. Although Vivian regained his health quickly, Harry struggled during his recovery. His legs, arms, and throat were paralyzed for months, and he was moved around in a baby carriage. At the time there was no antitoxin available to treat diphtheria. It took Harry about six months to get well, and he had to go to summer school to catch up on his lessons.

Harry wore glasses from the age of nine. This kept him from doing many things the

Harry wore eyeglasses beginning at the age of nine, which prevented him from participating in certain activities.

other boys did. He preferred to spend his time reading. Mark Twain, stories of the American Civil War, and the lives of great men were his favorites. He had read the Bible through twice before he was twelve. There was a small library in Independence where young Harry spent additional hours reading histories, novels, and encyclopedias. Sometimes he took the encyclopedias home with him to read. Mathilda Brown, Truman's high-school history teacher, said of him: "I doubt if there was a student in any high school in the country who knew more of the history of the United States than Harry did." The smartest boy in that graduating class of 1901, however, was Charles G. Ross. Ross later became President Truman's press secretary.

During the summers Harry, Vivian, and Mary Jane visited their grandparents, Harriet and Solomon Young, on their farm at Grandview. There they helped with the farm work, rode horses, and swam. From the age of thirteen Harry took piano lessons, first in Independence and later in Kansas City. He became a good amateur pianist. Truman later said he might have become a concert pianist if he had not gone into politics. When he became president, he often played the piano to relax from the cares of office. He also

The Truman Family Farm

In 1906 Truman, at age twenty-two, left his job at a Kansas City bank to labor on his family's farm. The farm covered about 600 acres (240 hectares) near Grandview. The seven-room farmhouse had no plumbing or electricity, which was very different from what Truman had become used to while living in Kansas City. Truman shared a bedroom with his brother, Vivian.

Truman worked for a decade on the family farm, which was set up in 1867 by his grandparents, Solomon and Harriet Young, near Grandview.

Every morning on the farm, Truman's day started with his father's call to milk the cows and feed the hogs, horses, and mules. When he was finished with those tasks, Truman helped his mother and sister cook in the kitchen. After breakfast, he spent the rest of the day doing chores or overseeing the work of farmhands. At night, after supper, the family read, talked, or listened to the piano that Truman, his sister, Mary Jane, or his mother played. When Truman's father died in 1914, Harry took over the management of the farm.

After World War I Truman and his family decided to sell the farm animals at auction. Later, in 1940, Truman's mother lost the farm to foreclosure and moved to another house in Grandview. Over the following years Truman and his family reacquired parcels of the original farmland. In 1955 and 1958 the Trumans sold much of the land to developers, who constructed a shopping center and homes there.

In 1980 the US Department of the Interior gave the state of Missouri money to buy the farmhouse and 5.25 acres (2.12 hectares) of land from Vivian Truman's sons. In 1994 the National Park Service obtained the property and made it part of the Harry S. Truman National Historic Site. Although the inside of the farmhouse is closed to the public, visitors can tour the grounds.

accompanied his daughter, Margaret, when she sang for White House visitors. Chopin and Mozart were his favorite composers.

EARLY JOBS

After graduation from high school, Harry tried for an appointment to the United States Military Academy at West Point, but he was rejected because of poor eyesight. Having no money to pay his way through college, he took a job in a Kansas City drugstore. (Truman would become the last president not to have earned a college degree.) After a brief stay in the drugstore, Truman became a clerk at the *Kansas City Star*. He then tried working as a timekeeper for a railroad construction gang and a clerk in a Kansas City bank.

In 1905 Truman joined the Missouri National Guard, becoming part of Battery B in Kansas City. This time he had memorized the eye chart to make sure his poor eyesight did not disqualify him during the physical exam.

Five years after he had left high school, Truman had grown tired of city life. In 1906 he returned to his father's farm, where he worked for the next ten years.

Chapter 2
A Soldier and a Politician

Truman was still a farmer when the United States entered World War I in 1917. Nearly thirty-three years old and with two tours in the National Guard behind him, he immediately volunteered. Returning to the United States in 1919, Truman tried his hand in business. When that venture failed, he made the move to politics.

Wartime Service

After the United States entered the war, Truman rejoined the Missouri National Guard and was called for a short period of training at the Field Artillery School at Fort Sill, Oklahoma. He went to France with the

Truman accepted a commission as first lieutenant of Battery F of the 129th Field Artillery in June 1917. Later he was put in command of Battery D.

35th Division in April 1918 and was soon promoted to captain. He commanded Battery D of the 129th Field Artillery, which fought in the Vosges, St-Mihiel, and Meuse-Argonne offensives. The men under his command came to be devoted to him. After the war he was commissioned a major in the Field Artillery Reserve. He would remain in the reserve for many years, eventually retiring with the rank of colonel.

Marriage

On June 28, 1919, Truman married Elizabeth "Bess" Wallace of Independence. They had met in elementary school and became childhood sweethearts. The two were engaged before Truman left for World War I, but they postponed the wedding until he returned home. The Trumans would have one child, Mary Margaret, born in 1924.

After his marriage, Truman invested all his savings in a Kansas City haberdashery, a men's clothing store. His business partner was Eddie Jacobson, an army friend. The store was successful for two years but failed in 1922, a victim of the postwar economic depression. Truman faithfully repaid his creditors, though it took him the next twelve years to do so.

From 1919 to 1922 Truman (*left*) was a partner in the Truman and Jacobson haberdashery in Kansas City. When the business failed, Truman went into politics.

Launching a Political Career

Following the failure of his haberdashery business, Truman decided to seek a job in politics. While he was in the army, Truman had been a close friend of James Pendergast, nephew of Tom Pendergast, the Democratic political boss of Kansas City. This friendship led to Truman's appointment as overseer of highways for Jackson County. After serving one year in that office Truman was elected judge in Jackson County in 1922, again with

Pendergast support. He was not required to be a lawyer to hold this job, but Truman felt that he would help his career if he studied law. So he enrolled in the Kansas City Law School and attended night classes for two years.

In 1924 Truman was defeated for reelection. "I was broke and out of a job with a family to support," Truman later said. "But I had a lot of friends and pulled through until 1926." That year he was elected presiding judge of the Jackson County Court. This was not a judicial job. In most states it would be called the chairman of the board of county commissioners. The job included the supervision of many county expenditures. Reelected in 1930, Truman was responsible for spending more than $60 million on highway and building construction. He built a reputation for efficiency and absolute honesty in contrast to the bad reputation of many of his political associates.

US Senator

In 1934 Truman was selected as the Pendergast candidate for United States senator. He won the Democratic nomination in a three-man race and was elected senator from Missouri, defeating the incumbent, Republican Roscoe

Truman holds his infant daughter, Mary Margaret (called Margaret), in the yard of the Trumans' home in Independence, Missouri. Margaret was born in 1924.

Harry S. Truman

Truman took office as a US senator in January 1935. He posed for this photograph at the US Capitol around 1940.

C. Patterson. In January 1935 Truman was sworn in as Missouri's junior senator by Vice President John Nance Garner.

Truman began his Senate career under the cloud of being a puppet of the corrupt Pendergast, but Truman's friendliness, personal honesty, and attention to the duties of his office soon won over his colleagues. He was responsible for two important pieces of legislation: the Civil Aeronautics Act of 1938, which established government regulation of the aviation industry, and the Wheeler-Truman Transportation Act of 1940, which provided government oversight of railroad reorganization.

After a challenging Democratic primary victory in 1940, Truman was reelected for a second term in the Senate. During this term he gained national recognition for leading an investigation into fraud and waste in the US military.

The Truman Committee

While the United States was preparing for war, Truman recalled the stories of federal waste during World War I. From the books he had read as a boy he also remembered the work

The Civil Aeronautics Act of 1938

As a US senator, Truman helped draft the Civil Aeronautics Act, which President Franklin D. Roosevelt signed into law in 1938. Before this law's passage, the airlines were regulated primarily by the Bureau of Air Commerce, a branch of the US Department of Commerce. The Civil Aeronautics Act transferred control of aviation from the Department of Commerce to a new independent agency, the Civil Aeronautics Authority (CAA). The CAA was responsible for making and enforcing rules for aircraft operations. It also had the power to regulate airline fares and to determine which routes airlines served. The Civil Aeronautics Act also established an Air Safety Board to investigate accidents and suggest ways to prevent them.

In 1940 President Roosevelt divided the CAA into two agencies, the Civil Aeronautics Administration and the Civil Aeronautics Board. In 1958 the tasks of the Civil Aeronautics Administration were transferred to the new Federal Aviation Agency. Later renamed as the Federal Aviation Administration, the organization still regulates US aviation today.

done by the famous Civil War Commission on the Conduct of the War. With these things in mind Senator Truman toured the country in his own car at his own expense to observe the progress of World War II work. The irregularities he saw during his 30,000-mile (48,000-kilometer) tour prompted him to ask

Senator Truman *(far right)* leads the Special Committee to Investigate the National Defense Program. The Truman Committee looked into federal contracts and purchases of munitions and airplane plants, among other issues.

the Senate to create the Special Committee to Investigate the National Defense Program, commonly called the Truman Committee.

The committee probed into many agencies and industries that produced war materials. It brought to light and helped to correct many cases of mismanagement, waste, and negligence. It saved the government an estimated $15 billion. Later, when fifty newspapermen voted on the ten men who had made the greatest contributions to the war effort, Truman was the only legislator on the list.

Chapter 3

First President from Missouri

In the summer of 1944, Truman was the junior senator from Missouri. Less than a year later, he was president of the United States. As vice president at the time of President Roosevelt's sudden death, Truman was thrust into the country's highest office at a pivotal moment. He had to lead the country through the final stages of World War II, in the process facing one of the most monumental presidential decisions in US history.

A Reluctant Candidate

At the Democratic National Convention in July 1944, a lively contest developed between several candidates for the vice presidential nomination. Most conspicuous were Henry Wallace, the incumbent vice president who had the support of the radical wing of the Democratic Party, and James Byrnes, a former senator and Supreme Court justice who represented the conservative wing. The deadlock was broken by naming Truman as the compromise candidate.

Truman at first flatly refused to take the nomination. He wanted to remain in the Senate. Roosevelt was not present at the convention because he was on his way to the South Pacific to discuss war strategy. On the telephone, Roosevelt was insistent. "Well," he said, "you can tell the senator that if he wants to break up the Democratic Party in the middle of the war, that's his responsibility." Truman finally agreed to accept the nomination.

THE CAMPAIGN AND ELECTION OF 1944

The general election campaign of 1944 pitted Roosevelt, who was running for a fourth term, and Truman against the Republicans Thomas E. Dewey, the governor of New York, and his vice presidential running mate, John W. Bricker. Dewey was the strongest campaigner Roosevelt had faced. After

At the Democratic National Convention of 1944 in Chicago, Senator Samuel D. Jackson of Indiana, chairman of the convention, brought Truman up to the microphone to speak after he was nominated as the vice presidential candidate.

endorsing the administration's general foreign and domestic policies and reforms, Dewey declared that the administration was dominated by "tired and quarrelsome old men." He challenged chiefly the management of the federal government and repeated that it was "time for a change."

Truman ran an admirable nationwide campaign, traveling from coast to coast. In the end, the Democrats won a comfortable victory, winning by nearly 3.6 million votes and capturing 432 electoral votes to the Republicans' 99. Despite the landslide, it was the closest of the four presidential elections that Roosevelt had won and his lowest number of electoral votes.

Truman, with his hand raised, takes the oath of office as vice president of the United States on January 20, 1945, on the south portico of the White House. Outgoing vice president Henry A. Wallace (*second from left*) administers the oath.

Succession to the Presidency

As vice president, Truman had little to do with shaping the country's policies at home or abroad. His chief task was presiding over the US Senate. President Roosevelt seldom consulted with him, and Truman met with the president only two times.

Roosevelt died suddenly of a cerebral hemorrhage on April 12, 1945, leaving Truman and the public in shock. Truman was sworn in as president on the same day. The new president faced many challenges. Presidential aides and others did their best to help him, and Truman learned quickly.

Two weeks after he became president, Truman learned of the Manhattan Project—the top-secret US project to develop an atomic bomb. On July 16, 1945, he was told a successful atom bomb test had been made at a site near Alamogordo, New Mexico, about 250 miles (400 km) south of Los Alamos, where the main laboratory complex was located. The blast from the bomb was equal to the force of about 40,000 pounds (18,000 kilograms) of dynamite—2,000 times greater than the most powerful bomb in existence at the time.

The first atomic bomb was detonated at the White Sands Missile Range in New Mexico at 5:30 a.m. on July 16, 1945. The code name of the bomb was Trinity.

The Potsdam Conference

The last Allied conference of World War II was held in Potsdam, a suburb of Berlin, Germany, from July 17 to August 2, 1945. It was attended by President Truman, British Prime Minister Winston Churchill, and Soviet Premier Joseph Stalin. During the conference Churchill would be replaced by Clement Attlee, who succeeded him as prime minister.

The Manhattan Project

The Manhattan Project was the largest scientific effort undertaken to that time. It involved thirty-seven installations throughout the country; at least thirteen university laboratories; and 100,000 people, including the Nobel prizewinning physicists Arthur Holly Compton, Enrico Fermi, Richard Feynman, Ernest Lawrence, and Harold Urey.

The origin of the Manhattan Project is often traced to a 1939 letter from the physicist Albert Einstein to President Franklin D. Roosevelt. The letter warned of German efforts to build a nuclear weapon and urged Roosevelt to appoint a committee to monitor nuclear developments. It was not until two years later, however, that Roosevelt took the step of ordering the Office of Scientific Research and Development, a government agency, to investigate the possibility of creating an atomic weapon. In 1942 the project was taken a step further when the Army Corps of Engineers was assigned the job of building facilities at which the research and testing would be carried out. This job was managed by the Corps of Engineers' Manhattan District, from which the project ultimately took its name.

From the beginning the Manhattan Project was shrouded in secrecy. Scientists worked in isolation, many of them in different parts of the country, unaware of the larger project in which they were involved. One of these scientists, the physicist J. Robert Oppenheimer, became concerned that the scientists' isolation from one another would jeopardize the project. He proposed the need for a central laboratory. Oppenheimer identified an isolated site at Los Alamos, New Mexico. When the site was approved, the Corps of Engineers began construction of a laboratory and compound in late 1942. In early 1943 Oppenheimer was appointed to head the laboratory.

The scientists at Los Alamos worked out the technology of the bomb itself, and elsewhere in the country citylike industrial complexes worked to produce enough U-235, a form of uranium, and plutonium to power the bomb. The largest of these complexes were at Oak Ridge, Tennessee, and on the Columbia River in Washington State.

The leaders discussed peace settlements for Europe but did not attempt to write peace treaties. That task was left to the Council of Foreign Ministers. The main concerns at Potsdam included the administration of defeated Germany and the continuing military campaign against Japan. The leaders also discussed the occupation of Austria, the borders of Poland, the determination of repayments for war damage, and the Soviet Union's role in Eastern Europe.

The Potsdam Conference's Declaration on Germany stated: "It is the intention of the

Prime Minister Winston Churchill of Great Britain, President Harry S. Truman, and Premier Joseph Stalin of the Soviet Union met at the Potsdam Conference in the summer of 1945. They discussed peace settlements and policy regarding postwar Europe.

Allies that the German people be given the opportunity to prepare for the eventual reconstruction of their life on a democratic and peaceful basis." The four occupation zones of Germany conceived at the Yalta Conference (February 1945) were set up—each to be administered by the commander-in-chief of the Soviet, British, United States, or French army of occupation. Berlin, Vienna, and Austria were also each divided into four occupation zones. Each Allied power was to take reparations from its own occupation zones. Poland's boundary was set at the Oder and Neisse rivers in the west, and the country received part of Germany's former East Prussia province. This required moving millions of Germans in those areas to Germany.

The Atomic Bomb

While in Potsdam, President Truman told Stalin about the "new weapon" (the atomic bomb) that the United States intended to use against Japan. An invasion of Japan had been in the planning stages for some time, but Truman wanted to avoid it. He consulted with his aides to decide whether the bomb should be used. They estimated that if the bomb worked it would save up to a million American lives. Truman suggested that the United States warn Japan that, if it did not surrender, the bomb would be used.

On July 26, 1945, Truman and the other Allied leaders issued the Potsdam Declaration, threatening "complete and utter destruction" of Japan if it did not unconditionally surrender. Japan refused to yield. On August 6, 1945, under Truman's orders, the United States dropped an atomic bomb, nicknamed Little Boy, on Hiroshima, shattering three-fifths

This photograph shows the aftermath of the explosion of the atomic bomb in Hiroshima, Japan, on August 6, 1945.

of the city. Three days later another bomb, called Fat Man, was dropped on Nagasaki. More than 100,000 people were killed in the two attacks. On August 10 Japan announced its intention to surrender, and it did so formally on September 2 (September 1 in the United States).

Chapter 4

Postwar Challenges

Japan's surrender officially ended World War II, but many challenges remained. At home, Truman faced labor issues and growing calls for equal rights for African Americans. Abroad, he confronted a new aggressiveness by the Soviet Union. Soviet efforts to spread communism in the postwar years began a tense rivalry between the United States and the Soviet Union that would influence world affairs for decades to come.

Joining the United Nations

During the early months of the Truman Administration, an international conference in San Francisco, California, had written a charter for a new peace organization, the United Nations. Truman was strongly in favor of the United States becoming a key member of this organization. He had always felt the United States had been wrong in failing to join the League of Nations after World War I. On July 28, 1945, the United States Senate approved the United Nations charter. In December 1945 the Senate and House of Representatives voted to place the United States in the United Nations.

President Truman signs the United Nations charter on August 8, 1945, while Secretary of State James F. Byrnes looks on. Truman's signature completed the ratification of the document by the United States.

Labor Problems at Home

The first crisis of the president's administration occurred shortly after his return to the United States from the Potsdam Conference late in 1945. Nationwide strikes threatened to disrupt the orderly return to normal business. By January 1946, 1.5 million workers had left their jobs in the automotive, electrical, meat, and steel industries. During April 1946, John L. Lewis led a strike of 400,000 members of the United Mine Workers. In May the railroad locomotive engineers and trainmen struck. Truman ordered government seizure of the mines and railroads. The rail strike lasted only two days. Late in May the government and the miners' union signed a contract ending the mine strike. From June 1946 on, Truman and his administration faced increasingly critical price and supply problems in such fields as housing, food, clothing, and automobiles. General dissatisfaction brought political disaster for the administration in the congressional elections on November 5, 1946. A Republican landslide swept the nation and the Republicans won control of both houses of Congress.

President Truman (*left*), Secretary of the Interior Julius Krug (*center*), and United Mine Workers chief John L. Lewis (*right*) meet to sign a work contract on May 29, 1946, ending a mining strike and government seizure of soft coal mines.

Before the new Congress met, Lewis ordered the United Mine Workers to strike on November 21. Angered, Truman gave instructions for a fight to the finish. The government obtained a federal court injunction, claiming interference with government operation of the mines. When Lewis ignored this, the Supreme Court found him guilty of contempt of court. He was fined $10,000 and his union, $700,000. Meanwhile, Lewis had called off the strike.

THE COLD WAR

In the postwar years Truman faced a new threat abroad—the Soviet Union's desire to extend communism into Europe and beyond. From 1945 to 1948 the Soviet Union strengthened its hold on Poland, Hungary, Romania, Bulgaria, Czechoslovakia, and East Germany. Truman addressed Soviet expansionism in a 1946 letter to Secretary of State James Byrnes. "Unless Russia is faced with an iron fist and strong language," he wrote, "another war is in the making." The rivalry that developed between the United States and the Soviet Union was known as the Cold War.

Truman Doctrine

In March 1947 Truman put the world on notice that the United States would oppose communist aggression throughout the world. Specifically, he called for economic and military aid to Greece and Turkey, both of which were threatened with communist takeover. Congress appropriated the money. This policy of aid to combat Soviet ambitions was popularly known as the Truman Doctrine. The US policy of blocking the expansionist policy of the Soviet Union was also called containment.

President Truman signs the Foreign Aid Assistance Act, which provided economic aid to Greece and Turkey in 1947 to help them resist communist aggression. This act introduced the policy known as the Truman Doctrine.

The Berlin Blockade and Airlift

After capturing Berlin during World War II, the Allies divided the city, as they had Germany, into four occupation zones. The French, British, and US zones were in western Berlin; the Soviet zone was in eastern Berlin. In March 1948 France, Great Britain, and the United States merged their zones into a single economic unit. The Soviet Union responded by beginning a blockade of all rail, road, and water communications between Berlin and the West. On June 24, 1948, the Soviets announced that the four-power administration of Berlin had ended and that the Allies no longer had any rights there.

German children cheer atop the ruins of a building in western Berlin as American and British forces bring in food and supplies during the Soviet blockade. The Soviets had hoped to push the West out of Berlin by cutting off all surface traffic to West Berlin.

On June 26 Truman approved a plan to supply West Berlin with vital supplies by air. US and British planes would eventually airlift more than 2.3 million tons of coal, food, and industrial goods to the city. Despite dire shortages of fuel and electricity, the airlift kept life going in West Berlin for eleven months, until on May 12, 1949, the Soviet Union lifted the blockade. As a result of the blockade and airlift, Berlin became a symbol of the Allies' willingness to oppose further Soviet expansion.

Marshall Plan

On June 5, 1947, Secretary of State George C. Marshall proposed an even stronger measure to combat communism. The Marshall Plan, officially called the European Recovery Program, would provide financial aid to help rebuild European economies devastated by the war. The goal was to create stable conditions in those countries and thereby enable them to resist communist aggression. The Marshall Plan originally offered aid to all European countries. The Soviet Union prevented the countries of Eastern Europe from accepting any aid, however, so the program was confined to the nations of Western Europe.

The Marshall Plan was signed into law by President Truman on April 3, 1948. Over the next four years, the United States distributed more than $13 billion worth of economic aid, helping to restore industrial and agricultural production, establish financial stability, and expand trade. Direct grants accounted for the vast majority of the aid, with the remainder in the form of loans.

The Marshall Plan was very successful. The Western European countries involved experienced a rise in their gross national products of 15 to 25 percent during this period. The plan contributed greatly to the rapid renewal of the Western European chemical, engineering, and steel industries. It also achieved its goal of preventing the spread of communism into Western Europe.

Taft-Hartley and Other Acts of Congress

During 1947 the Republican Eightieth Congress passed the Labor-Management Relations Act over the president's veto. Commonly known as the Taft-Hartley Act, the law preserved the rights of labor to organize and to bargain collectively. It also guaranteed employees the right not to join unions and permitted union shops only where state law allowed and where a majority of workers voted for them. The act required unions to give sixty days' advance notice of a strike and authorized eighty-day federal injunctions when a strike threatened to imperil national health or safety. It also narrowed the definition of unfair labor practices, specified unfair union practices, restricted union political contributions, and required union officers to deny under oath any communist affiliations.

On June 20, 1947, Truman delivered a radio address explaining his reasons for vetoing the bill, stating in part:

> *The bill is deliberately designed to weaken labor unions. When the sponsors of the bill claim that weakening unions, they are giving rights back to individual workingmen, they ignore the basic reason why unions are important in our democracy. Unions exist so that laboring men can bargain with their employers on a basis of equality. Because of unions, the living standards of our working people have increased steadily until they are today the highest in the world.*

Congress passed the bill during a period of growing opposition to labor unions after World War II. At the time there was a fear of communist infiltration of unions, a tremendous growth in both membership and power of unions, and a series of large-scale strikes.

Another domestic issue acted on by Congress was the line of succession to the presidency. The line of succession determines who will become president if the office becomes vacant. The US Constitution, as adopted in 1789, established that the vice president is first in line. The Presidential Succession Act of 1792 placed the president pro tempore of the Senate (who presides over the Senate in the absence of the vice president) second in line, followed by the speaker of the House. In 1886 Congress removed the president pro tempore and the speaker of the House from the line of succession and replaced them with members of the president's Cabinet, who are appointed by the president rather than elected to office. During Truman's presidency, at his request, Congress again revised the line of succession. The Presidential Succession Act of 1947 reinstalled the original elected officials in line after the vice president but moved the speaker of the House ahead of the president pro tempore of the Senate. The line of succession then continued with various Cabinet members, led by the secretary of state. The act made it less likely that a nonelected official would become president.

Also in 1947 Truman signed into law the National Security Act. This act reorganized the structure of the US armed forces, combining the former War and Navy departments into a new National Military Establishment (later called the US Department of Defense). It created the office of secretary of defense to oversee the military, and it created the National Security Council and separate departments for each branch of the armed forces. It enabled the coordination of the military with other departments and agencies of the government that were concerned with national security, such as the Central Intelligence Agency, which the act also created. It also provided for presidential and congressional oversight with respect to matters of national intelligence.

Truman and the Civil Rights Movement

On December 5, 1946, Truman established the President's Committee on Civil Rights by Executive Order 9808. He wanted the committee to suggest measures to strengthen and safeguard the civil rights of the American people. After World War II African Americans who had served in the military were demanding the right to vote, a right that was being denied to them in the Southern states.

Truman urged the committee to right this wrong by recommending which laws needed to be changed or strengthened.

On June 29, 1947, Truman became the first president to address the National Association for the Advancement of Colored People (NAACP), the country's most prominent civil rights organization. He spoke to members of the NAACP at the Lincoln Memorial in Washington, DC. In his speech, which was broadcast nationally over the radio, Truman urged the federal government to lead in the fight to guarantee the civil rights of all Americans.

Truman continued to promote civil rights in his State of the Union message to Congress on January 7, 1948, in which he said:

> *The United States has always had a deep concern for human rights. Religious freedom, free speech, and freedom of thought are cherished realities in our land. Any denial of human rights is a denial of the basic beliefs of democracy and of our regard for the worth of each individual.*
>
> *Today, however, some of our citizens are still denied equal opportunity for education, for jobs and economic advancement,*

and for the expression of their views at the polls. Most serious of all, some are denied equal protection under laws. Whether discrimination is based on race, or creed, or color, or land of origin, it is utterly contrary to American ideals of democracy.

On June 29, 1947, President Truman addressed a conference of the National Association for the Advancement of Colored People at the Lincoln Memorial.

In a special message to Congress on February 2, 1948, Truman spoke again of civil rights. In this speech he listed ten objectives for furthering civil rights in the United States and recommended that Congress pass laws so that these goals could be reached. The objectives included making the President's Committee on Civil Rights a permanent commission, strengthening existing civil rights laws, enacting a federal law against lynching, protecting the right to vote, creating a commission to stop unfair discrimination in employment, and preventing discrimination in interstate transportation facilities.

Although his efforts to push a civil rights bill through Congress were blocked in the Senate by powerful Southern leaders, Truman signed two executive orders on July 26, 1948. Executive Order 9980 established fair employment practices in the civilian agencies of the federal government. Executive Order 9981 desegregated the US military. It instructed the US armed forces to provide "equality of treatment and opportunity for all personnel without regard to race, color, religion, or national origin" and provided for a presidential committee to oversee that the order was carried out.

Chapter 5

A Second Term

As the presidential election of 1948 approached, the odds against Truman's winning the presidency seemed enormous. The Republicans had triumphed in the congressional elections of 1946, running against Truman as the symbol of the New Deal. That electoral triumph seemed to indicate that the American people were weary of reform and of the Democratic Party. But, in the end, Truman surprised everyone to win a second term. The chief event of his second term was the Korean War.

A Fighting Campaign Brings Victory

In June 1948 the Republicans nominated Governor Thomas E. Dewey of New York for president. Many Democratic leaders tried to avoid Truman's leadership by pressing the nomination of General Dwight D. Eisenhower. Eisenhower refused to be considered, and the Democrats nominated Truman. Senator Alben Barkley of Kentucky was his running mate.

President Truman (*center*) shakes the hand of his running mate, Senator Alben Barkley, at the start of his 1948 campaign whistle-stop train tour. Standing with them is Truman's wife, Bess.

A group of Southern Democrats, enraged by Truman's civil rights program, revolted and held a convention in Birmingham, Alabama. They formed their own party and called it the States' Rights Democratic Party, nicknamed the "Dixiecrats." They nominated Senator J. Strom Thurmond of South Carolina as the States' Rights Democratic candidate for president. Another threat to Truman arose from the formation of a Progressive Party, with Henry Wallace as its candidate for the presidency.

All political indications pointed to a Republican landslide. Truman, however, refused to believe the public opinion polls. He launched a cross-country whistle-stop train trip, railing against the "do-nothing, good-for-nothing Republican Congress." He traveled more than 30,000 miles (48,000 km) and made some 300 speeches in more than 250 cities. He hammered away at Republican support for the antilabor Taft-Hartley Act and other conservative policies. Crowds responded enthusiastically, shouting "Give 'em hell, Harry!" The excitement generated by Truman's energetic campaigning contrasted sharply with Dewey's lackluster speeches.

A Second Term

As the returns rolled in on the night of the election, November 2, Truman took a narrow lead. However, political commentators still believed that Dewey would ultimately win. Indeed, the *Chicago Daily Tribune* distributed a newspaper with the now-famous headline "Dewey Defeats Truman." The *Tribune* was not alone that night in its error. In the end, Truman achieved one of the most dramatic political upsets in the nation's history. He was the first Democratic president to be elected without the "solid South." He won 28 states

Truman holds up a copy of the *Chicago Daily Tribune* with the headline "Dewey Defeats Truman." Despite what the newspaper had printed, Truman won the 1948 election with a larger margin of victory over Thomas E. Dewey than Franklin D. Roosevelt had achieved in 1944.

and 303 electoral votes. The Democrats also won control of Congress. Dewey carried 16 states, winning 189 electoral votes; Thurmond won 4 states and 39 electoral votes.

Truman's Fair Deal and Other Domestic Affairs

In January 1949 Truman reasserted his domestic reform proposals under the catchphrase Fair Deal. It included proposals for expanded public housing, increased aid to education, a higher minimum wage, federal protection for civil rights, and national health insurance. The economy-minded Eighty-first Congress would agree to legislate only a few of the president's recommendations: it raised the minimum wage, promoted slum clearance, and extended old-age benefits to an additional ten million people.

Major strikes in the coal, steel, and automobile industries continued to threaten the nation's economy as Truman's second term began. Another problem was communism at home. In October 1949 eleven American communist leaders were fined and sentenced to prison terms for conspiracy against the government. Charges were soon made that there were communists in the State Department, though a Senate subcommittee later cleared the department. In September 1950 Congress passed a strict communist-control bill over Truman's veto.

In 1950 the Eighty-first Congress enlarged the Displaced Persons Act of 1948 to admit more than 415,000 refugees to the United States. In the same year it also broadened the Social Security program and extended rent control. Increased defense appropriations were made for producing the hydrogen bomb, which Truman had ordered. The air force was installing a radar-warning screen around the United States and Alaska.

In 1951 the Twenty-second Amendment was added to the Constitution. It limited a president to two full terms or to a total of ten years if he had served part of an unexpired term. (The amendment did not apply to Truman; he was free to run for a second full term in 1952 if he chose.) The amendment had been passed in 1947 by a Republican Congress, mostly as a reaction against Franklin D. Roosevelt's four presidential election victories. It has been argued that this controversial amendment serves

President Truman leaves Blair House, where he and his family lived while the White House was renovated during his second term.

to weaken a president's effectiveness during the second term, because the incumbent cannot run for reelection.

During Truman's second term, the White House was renovated. He had had an inspection done on the White House during the winter of 1947. The inspectors found that the second floor of the White House living quarters as well as the ceiling in the state dining room were very unstable. Between 1948 and 1952 the White House had to be completely reconstructed. During most of this period the Truman family lived at Blair House, across the street from the Executive Mansion. In 1950 Truman survived an assassination attempt that took place there.

Assassination Attempt

On November 1, 1950, Truman was taking an afternoon nap in a second-floor bedroom at Blair House when an attempt on his life occurred. Oscar Collazo and Griselio Torresola, who were activists in the Puerto Rican independence movement, tried to shoot their way to the front door. White House police officers and Secret Service agents engaged in a shootout with the men in front of the building. Truman awoke when he heard the gunfire. He ran to the front window, but a guard yelled to him to duck down and protect himself. Three police officers were injured, Torresola was killed, and Collazo was wounded. Leslie Coffelt, one of the police officers who had been shot, died later that day.

 Truman took the attempt on his life calmly, keeping all the rest of his scheduled appointments that day and going for his customary early-morning walk the following day. He was familiar with the fact that Abraham Lincoln, James A. Garfield, and William McKinley were murdered while in office and that assassins had tried to kill Andrew Jackson, Theodore Roosevelt, and Franklin Roosevelt. "A president has to expect such things," Truman said. His would-be assassins were members of the Puerto Rican revolutionary Nationalist Party determined to obtain Puerto Rican independence. Collazo was convicted of murdering Coffelt and sentenced to die in the electric chair. Truman later commuted the sentence to life imprisonment. The president had previously assured the Puerto Rican people they were free to work out their own political future.

War in Korea

On June 25, 1950, military forces of communist North Korea invaded noncommunist South Korea, setting off the Korean War. This was a great personal blow to Truman. He had often said he wanted more than anything else to be regarded by historians as a president who brought peace to the world. Truman ordered US military forces to support the United Nations "police action" in Korea. On December 16 he declared a state of national emergency to help prepare the United States for a possible "all-out" war with communism.

When Chinese troops rushed in to back the North Koreans, General Douglas MacArthur, commander of the United Nations forces, wanted to strike directly at China in an effort to win a quick victory. Truman insisted on confining the fight to Korea. On April 11, 1951, Truman relieved MacArthur of all his commands and replaced him with General Matthew Ridgway. MacArthur immediately returned home. He received tremendous acclaim for his heroic services in World War II and in Korea. Ridgway later became Supreme Commander, Allied Powers in Europe, succeeding General

Dwight D. Eisenhower in that post in June 1952. Eisenhower then came home to seek the Republican presidential nomination.

On the home front the nation worked to rearm itself and its Allies. Before the outbreak of fighting in Korea, the United States was devoting 6 percent of its industrial production to national defense. By 1952 it had climbed to 20 percent of all production in the midst of a growing peacetime economic expansion. The cost of living, by the summer of 1951, had soared to more than 185 percent of the base average of 1935–39, and prices had climbed about 9 percent since 1950.

In July 1950, during the Korean War, American soldiers fire a howitzer gun against North Korean invaders. Truman agonized over his decision to enter the Korean conflict.

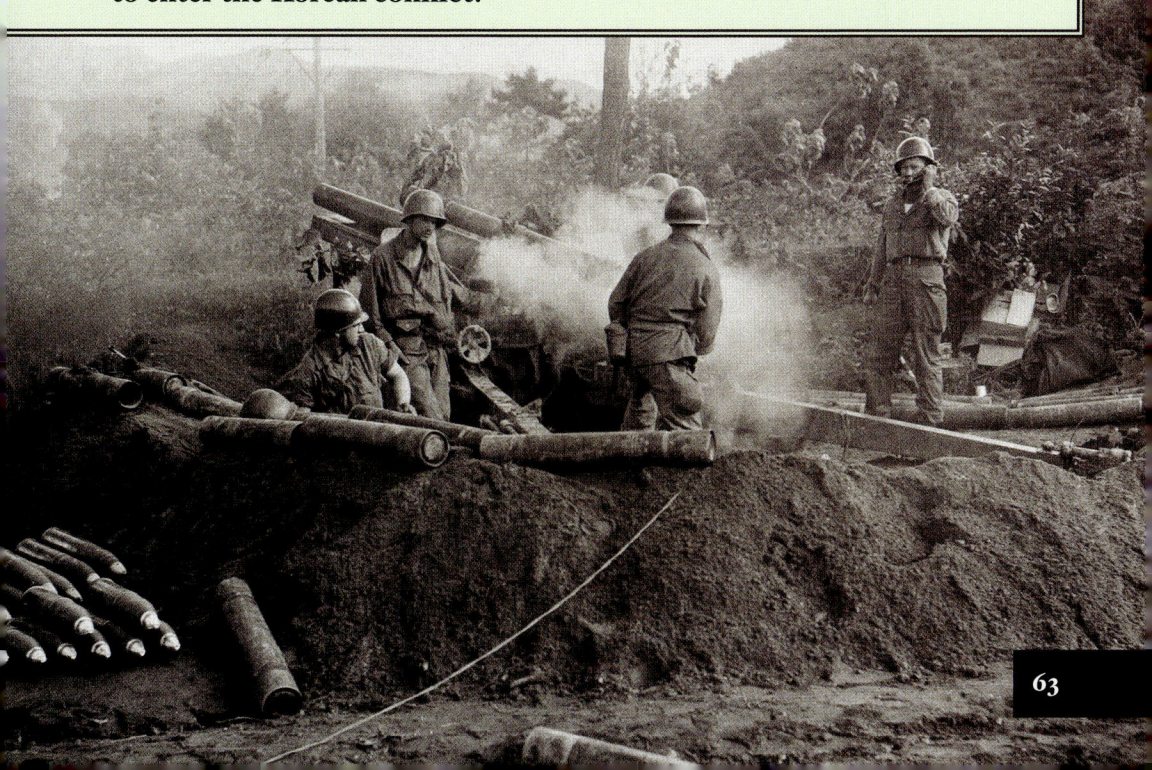

An Active Political Career Comes to a Close

A big problem facing Truman in 1952 was the charge of corruption in the federal government. In the previous year congressional investigations had turned up irregularities in several government departments. Truman instructed the attorney general's department to weed out dishonest officials.

During its second session the Eighty-first Congress ratified the peace treaty with Japan and approved a "peace contract" with West Germany. To strengthen national defense, Congress appropriated more than $6 billion for the second year of the Mutual Security Program and more than $46 billion for the armed forces. Congress also passed a "GI Bill of Rights" for Korean War veterans.

A blow to defense production in 1952 was a fifty-four-day strike by the C.I.O. United Steelworkers. At first Truman averted the strike when he ordered the government to take over ninety-two steel companies. The Supreme Court ruled the action unconstitutional and the workers went out on strike at once. The dispute was finally settled with an overall wage increase.

A Second Term

Truman refused to seek reelection in 1952, and the Democratic nomination went to Governor Adlai E. Stevenson of Illinois. The candidate for the Republican Party was General Dwight D. Eisenhower. The election campaign was one of the most vigorous in the country's history. Truman himself made three whistle-stop tours on behalf of Stevenson. On November 4 Eisenhower was overwhelmingly elected.

Conclusion

Eisenhower was inaugurated on January 20, 1953, and Truman retired to his home in Independence, Missouri. When he left office, Truman said, "I have had a career from precinct to president, and I'm proud of that career." Friends raised funds to build the Harry S. Truman Library in Independence.

Truman's life in retirement was modest but active, typified by his habit of taking a brisk morning walk, or "constitutional," along the sidewalks of Independence. He

Former president Truman stands in front of the Harry S. Truman Library in Independence, Missouri, in 1960. The Truman Library was the first presidential library to be established under the terms of the 1955 Presidential Libraries Act.

Conclusion

enjoyed joking with reporters. He remained in good health, spending his days reading, until the mid-1960s, when his health declined quickly. On Christmas Day 1972, Truman lapsed into unconsciousness, and he died the next morning.

Truman was buried in the courtyard of the Harry S. Truman Library. His memoirs appeared in 1955–56. In 1959 his birthplace at Lamar was dedicated as a Missouri state shrine. In 1965 the Medicare act—government health insurance for the aged, first sponsored by Truman in 1945—was signed by President Lyndon B. Johnson in the Truman Library.

Although Truman left office with low public approval, his standing among US presidents rose in later years. He began to be appreciated as a president who had, in Truman's own words, "done his damnedest." A common man thrust into leadership at a critical time in the country's history, Truman had risen to the challenge and performed far better than nearly everyone had expected.

Glossary

affiliation A close connection with or to something.

aggression The practice of making attacks; hostile or destructive behavior.

appropriate To set apart for a particular purpose or use.

avert To keep from happening.

blockade A barrier to the passage of people, supplies, or communications in or out of a country or city.

cerebral hemorrhage Bleeding from a ruptured blood vessel in the brain that is often life-threatening.

commission To give someone a military rank.

common sense The ability to think and behave in a reasonable way and to make good decisions.

conservative Believing in the value of established and traditional practices in politics and society.

containment Actions that are intended to keep an unfriendly government from getting more power.

Glossary

discrimination The treating of some people better than others without any fair or proper reason.

expenditure An amount of money that is spent on something.

foreclosure The act of taking back property because the money owed for the property has not been paid.

haberdashery A store selling men's clothing and accessories.

inaugurate To introduce into office with a formal ceremony.

infiltration The act of entering or becoming established gradually or secretly.

injunction A court order commanding or forbidding some act.

negligence Failure to take the care that a responsible person usually takes.

radical Favoring rapid and sweeping changes especially in laws and methods of government.

reparations Money or materials paid by a country that loses a war to the winner to make up for damages done in the war.

segregation The separation or isolation of a race, class, or group.

succession The order, action, or right of succeeding to a title or property.

veto The power of a person in authority to prevent a bill passed by a legislature from becoming law.

For More Information

Bradbury Science Museum
1350 Central Avenue
Los Alamos, NM 87544
(505) 667-4444
Website: http://www.lanl.gov/museum
This museum displays a collection of historical weapons-research artifacts from Los Alamos National Laboratory. The laboratory was a key site for the Manhattan Project during World War II.

Harry S. Truman Library and Museum
500 West US Highway 24
Independence, MO 64050
(816) 268-8200
Website: http://www.trumanlibrary.org
This presidential library, administered by the National Archives and Records Administration, makes Truman's papers

For More Information

and other research materials accessible for study. The museum exhibits artifacts and photographs from Truman's personal life and his administration. To study documents about the Berlin Airlift, see https://www.trumanlibrary.org/whistlestop/study_collections/berlin_airlift/large/.

Harry S. Truman National Historic Site
223 North Main Street
Independence, MO 64050
(816) 254-2720
Website: https://www.nps.gov/hstr/index.htm
The Truman Home in Independence is operated by the National Park Service. Built by Bess Truman's grandfather in 1867, it was the home the Trumans lived in after they were married in 1919.

The Harry S. Truman Scholarship Foundation
712 Jackson Place NW
Washington, DC 20006
(202) 395-4831
Website: http://www.truman.gov
This foundation is dedicated to encouraging

young leaders and provides scholarships to students for graduate studies in public service. It offers a weeklong program for each new class of Truman Scholars to help them improve leadership skills.

Miller Center of Public Affairs
PO Box 400406
Charlottesville, VA 22904
(434) 924-7236
Website: http://millercenter.org/president/truman
This institute at the University of Virginia focuses on presidential studies, history, and public policy. Its website contains information about Truman's life, presidency, and legacy.

The National Archives and Records Administration (NARA)
8601 Adelphi Road
College Park, MD 20740-6001
(866) 272-6272
Website: http://www.archives.gov
NARA is the keeper of the nation's records—all the documents and materials that are created during the course of the federal government's daily business,

For More Information

including acts of Congress, presidential proclamations, and executive orders. The website contains searchable databases of US historical documents, such as Truman's 1947 message to Congress in which he recommended assistance to Greece and Turkey, which introduced the Truman Doctrine (http://www.archives.gov/historical-docs/todays-doc/?dod-date=312). NARA also oversees the Presidential Library system.

State Historical Society of Missouri
Columbia Research Center
1020 Lowry Street
Columbia, MO 65201-7298
(800) 747-6366
Website: http://shsmo.org
This organization is the primary research center for Missouri's state and local history. Its website presents biographies of notable Missourians, including Harry S. Truman (http://shsmo.org/historicmissourians/name/t/trumanh/).

United Nations
Website: http://www.un.org
The United Nations is an international

organization that was created in 1945. Today it has more than 190 member countries. Its chief divisions are the General Assembly, the Security Council, the Economic and Social Council, the Trusteeship Council, the International Court of Justice, and the Secretariat. The UN's website provides information on the history of the organization, the UN Charter, and programs for students.

Websites

Because of the changing nature of internet links, Rosen Publishing has developed an online list of Web sites related to the subject of this book. This site is updated regularly. Please use this link to access the list:

http://www.rosenlinks.com/PPPL/truman

For Further Reading

Boulware, Beverly Joan. *Harry and Eddie: The Friendship that Changed the World*. Nashville, TN: Harry & Eddie Publishing, 2015.

Docalavich, Heather. *The History, Structure, and Reach of the United Nations* (The United Nations: Leadership and Challenges in a Global World). Philadelphia, PA: Mason Crest Publishers, 2016.

Etingoff, Kim. *Harry Truman: From Farmer to President* (Extraordinary Success with a High School Diploma or Less). Philadelphia, PA: Mason Crest Publishers, 2013.

George, Enzo. *The Civil Rights Movement* (Primary Sources in U.S. History). New York, NY: Cavendish Square Publishing, 2016.

Griffel, Steven Jay. *Harry S. Truman: American President*. Upper Saddle River, NJ: Pearson Education, 2013.

Hajeski, Nancy J. *The Big Book of Presidents: From George Washington to Barack Obama*. New York, NY: Skyhorse Publishing, 2015.

Immell, Myra. *The McCarthy Era* (Perspectives on Modern World History). Detroit, MI: Greenhaven Press, 2011.

Mara, Wil. *Harry Truman* (Presidents and Their Times). New York, NY: Marshall Cavendish Benchmark, 2012.

Prentzas, G. S. *The Marshall Plan* (Milestones in World History). New York, NY: Chelsea House Publishers, 2011.

Roesler, Jill. *Eyewitness to the Dropping of the Atomic Bombs*. Mankato, MN: The Child's World, 2016.

Seth, Shaun, ed. *Key Figures of the Korean War* (Biographies of War). New York, NY: Britannica Educational Publishing, 2016.

Smibert, Angie. *12 Incredible Facts About the Dropping of the Atomic Bombs* (Turning Points in US History). North Mankato, MN: Peterson Publishing, 2016.

Uebelhor, Tracy S. *The Truman Years* (Presidential Profiles). New York, NY: Facts on File, 2006.

Wallenfeldt, Jeffrey H., ed. *A New World Power: America from 1920 to 1945* (Documenting America). New York, NY: Britannica Educational Publishing, 2013.

Ziff, John. *The Korean War* (Major U.S. Historical Wars). Philadelphia, PA: Mason Crest Publishers, 2016.

Index

A

atomic bomb, 7, 32, 34, 36–38

B

Barkley, Alben, 55
Berlin Blockade, 45

C

Central Intelligence Agency, 50
Churchill, Winston, 33
Civil Aeronautics Act of 1938, 25, 26
civil rights, 50–53, 55
Cold War, 8, 43–47
Collazo, Oscar, 61
communism, 8, 9, 39, 43, 46, 48, 58–59, 62
containment, 44
corruption, in federal government, 64

D

desegregation, of US military, 53
Dewey, Thomas, 29, 31, 55, 56, 57, 58
Displaced Persons Act of 1948, 59

E

Eisenhower, Dwight D., 55, 63, 65, 66
Executive Order 9980, 53
Executive Order 9981, 53

F

Fair Deal, 58

G

Germany, 8, 35, 36, 45, 64
"GI Bill of Rights," 64

H

Harry S. Truman Library, 66, 67
Harry S. Truman National Historic Site, 16
Hiroshima, bombing of, 8, 37

J

Japan, 7, 8, 35, 36–38, 39, 64

K

Korean War, 9, 54, 62, 63, 64

L

labor unions, 41, 43, 47, 48, 58, 64

M

MacArthur, Douglas, 62
Manhattan Project, 32, 34
Marshall Plan, 46
Missouri, 10, 13, 15, 16, 17, 20, 21–22, 25, 28, 66, 67

N

Nagasaki, bombing of, 8, 37
National Association for the Advancement of Colored People (NAACP), 51
National Security Act, 49–50
National Security Council, 50

P

peace treaties, 64
Potsdam Conference, 33, 35–36
Potsdam Declaration, 37
presidential elections
    of 1944, 29, 31
    of 1948, 54, 55–58
    of 1952, 65
presidential succession, 11, 48–49
Presidential Succession Act of 1947, 49
President's Committee on Civil Rights, 50, 52

R

reparations, 36
Ridgway, Matthew, 62
Roosevelt, Franklin D., 7, 26, 28, 29, 31, 32, 34, 59, 61

S

Soviet Union, 8, 35, 43, 44, 45, 46
Stalin, Joseph, 33, 36, 39
States' Rights Democratic Party (Dixiecrats), 56

T

Taft-Hartley Act, 47–48, 56
term limits, 59–60
Thurmond, Strom, 56, 58
Torresola, Griselio, 61
Truman, Harry
    assassination attempt, 60, 61
    childhood, 10, 13, 15
    child, 17, 20
    education, 13, 15, 17, 22
    death, 67
    early political career, 21–22
    as farmer, 16, 17, 18
    first term as president, 7–8, 13, 28, 32–33, 35–38, 39–41, 43–54
    marriage, 20
    military career, 17, 18, 20
    parents, 10–11, 13, 15, 16
    presidential campaign of 1948, 54, 55–58
    retirement, 66–67
    second term as president, 58–65
    as senator, 22, 25–27, 28
    as vice president, 7, 32
Truman Committee, 27
Truman Doctrine, 8, 44
Twenty-second Amendment, 59–60

U

United Nations, 9, 40

W

Wheeler-Truman Transportation Act, 25
World War I, 16, 18, 20, 25
World War II, 7, 8, 26, 28, 32–38, 39, 45, 48, 50, 62